Mary Cassatt

Edited by Lacey Belinda Smith

Portrait Of The Artist—1878--Impressionism

Mary Stevenson Cassatt (1844 – 1926) was an American painter and printmaker born in Allegheny City—now part of Pittsburgh, Pennsylvania. Mary Cassatt was one of the leading artists in the Impressionist movement of the later part of the 1800s. Cassatt often created images of the social and private lives of women especially with children.

Sketch Of Mrs. Currey—1871—Realism

The Mandolin Player—1872--Realism

During Carnival—1872-- Realism

Portrait Of A Woman—1872-- Realism

Bacchante—1872-- Realism

The Flirtation A Balcony In Seville—1872-- Realism

Offering The Panel To The Bullfighter--1872-1873-- Realism

Portrait Of A Lady Of Seville—1873-- Realism

Spanish Dancer Wearing A Lace Mantilla—1873-- Realism

Peasant Woman Peeling An Orange—1875-- Realism

Musical Party—1874-- Realism

Profile Of An Italian Woman—1873-- Impressionism

The Young Bride—1875--Realism

Mary Ellison Embroidering—1877-- Realism

The Opera--1877-1878--Realism

Head Of A Young Girl—1876--Impressionism

At The Theater--1878-1879--Impressionism

In The Box—1879--Impressionism

The Reader—1878--Impressionism, Realism

Theater—1879--Impressionism

The Cup Of Tea—1879--Impressionism

Woman Reading--1878-1879-- Impressionism

Woman With A Pearl Necklace—1879--Impressionism

Woman Reading In A Garden—1880--Impressionism

Woman In Black—1882--Impressionism

Woman Standing, Holding A Fan--1878-1879-- Impressionism

Maternity—1890--Impressionism

The Bath--1890-1891--Japonism

The Coiffure Study--1890-1891-- Impressionism, Japonism

The Lamp--1890-1891--Impressionism, Japonism

The Banjo Lesson—1893-- Impressionism, Japonism

Young Woman Sewing In The Garden--1880-1882-- Impressionism

The Letter--1890-1891--Japonism

Louise Nursing Her Child—1898-- Impressionism

Mother Jeanne Nursing Her Baby--1907-1908-- Impressionism

Celeste In A Brown Hat—1891--Impressionism

Summertime—1894--Impressionism

Sketch Of Antoinette (No.1)—1901--Impressionism

The Boating Party--1893-1894--Impressionism

Portrait Of A Young Woman In Green—1898-- Impressionism

Young Woman In Green Outdoors In The Sun—1914-- Impressionism

Mother And Two Children—1906--Impressionism

Mother About To Wash—1880-- Impressionism

Susan Seated Outdoors Wearing A Purple Hat—1881--Impressionism

Self Portrait—1880-- Impressionism

Emmie And Her Child—1889-- Impressionism

www.ingramcontent.com/pod-product-compliance
Lightning Source LLC
Chambersburg PA
CBHW050435180526
45159CB00006B/2551